F4

The High Achievers Handbook

By David Wible

To all those striving for a balanced and fulfilling life, this handbook is dedicated to you.

Table of Contents

Introduction	4
Chapter 1 - The Moment of Clarity	9
Chapter 2 - Building Your Vision: Turning Dreams into Action	11
Chapter 3 - Building Your Plan	19
Chapter 4 - Logging Your Activity	23
Chapter 5 - The System - The Central Hub	27
Chapter 6 - The Art of Alignment	33
Chapter 7 - Unleashing Your Superpowers	38
Chapter 8 - How to Delegate Activities	43
Chapter 9 - Success Begins with Fitness	48
Chapter 10 - Focus: The Discipline of Taking Time	54
Chapter 11 - The Importance of Fraternity	58
Chapter 12 - Financial Well-Being	65
Chapter 13 - Overcoming Challenges Implementing the F4	70
Chapter 14 - The HAF+ Time Report: Staying on Course	76
Chapter 15 - The Journey to M.A.P. - Finding the Right Course	83
Chapter 16 - Sustaining Long-Term Success with the F4 Framework	89
Acknowledgements	94

Introduction

"The only limit to our realization of tomorrow is our doubts of today." -Franklin D. Roosevelt

In August 2020, I found myself at the pinnacle of my career. I had just sold my company for an amount that ensured I would never have to work another day in my life if I chose not to. It was a moment that should have been filled with elation and triumph, marking the culmination of years of relentless hard work and dedication. Yet, as the initial excitement faded, I was left staring at a blank screen that had once been filled with countless business tasks, now replaced by an empty void.

Despite my business successes, I realized there was a profound imbalance in my life. The excitement of closing this major deal quickly gave way to a sense that something was missing. The pandemic had isolated us all, but this feeling went beyond that. I felt like I had no purpose anymore.

During the early days of my career, my focus had been singular: building a successful business. I dedicated countless hours to my work, driven by the pursuit of success and believing that achieving financial freedom would bring me the fulfillment I desired. But now, with financial stability achieved, I was confronted with a new issue. The one big thing that had dictated my hours each day was gone, leaving me with a deep sense of emptiness.

Determined to understand the root cause of this feeling, I embarked on a path of self-discovery. I began to read extensively on topics related to personal development, health, and well-being. I attended workshops, sought advice from mentors, and started to reflect deeply on my own life choices. I had always engaged in these activities, but I intensified my focus, weeding out what wasn't effective and identifying what was missing.

During this period of introspection, I came across a concept that would eventually become the foundation of my new life philosophy: the F4 framework. This simple yet profound framework emphasized the importance of balancing four key pillars in life: Fitness, Focus, Fraternity, and Finance.

The more I delved into these concepts, the more I realized how interconnected they were. True fulfillment, I discovered, comes from nurturing all four pillars, not just one. This realization was a turning point for me. I began to make deliberate changes in my life, prioritizing my physical health, mental clarity, relationships, and financial well-being in a balanced and holistic manner.

- **Fitness:** Although I had always worked out and preferred home workouts, I began to challenge myself by signing up for longer events that incorporated elevation and distance, sometimes spanning several days. My main goal was to show up regardless of how I felt, pushing myself both physically and mentally.
- **Focus:** I developed a focus routine that included reading, stretching, and meditation. These practices helped me clear my mind, set intentions, and maintain mental clarity, allowing me to approach challenges with a calm and strategic mindset.
- **Fraternity:** I realized the importance of strong relationships and the human mind's capacity to manage about 150 contacts. I viewed my engagement with people as more social than opportunistic, striving to provide more value than I took. Using the Relate Matrix, I prioritized

reconnecting with friends and expanding my network. My wife, DaniElle, and I made a concerted effort to divide up actions needed to make our life, home, and family amazing.
- **Finance:** Despite my financial stability, I knew I needed to refine my approach to managing wealth and investments. My financial advisor, John, played a crucial role in guiding me through this process. Together, we created a comprehensive financial plan that focused on reducing debt, increasing savings, and making strategic investments. This proactive approach to finance not only provided peace of mind but also empowered me to make informed decisions about my future.

One of the most transformative aspects of my journey was the realization of the power of accountability. I found accountability partners who provided honest feedback and support, offering tough love when needed and celebrating my successes. This dynamic was instrumental in pushing me to stay committed to my goals and continuously improve.

Understanding the **G.A.P.** (Goals, Accountability, Process) was a game-changer. By clearly defining my goals, identifying accountability partners, and outlining a detailed process, I gained clarity and direction. This structured approach enabled me to take actionable steps towards my aspirations, even when faced with obstacles. The G.A.P. framework became a vital tool in my journey towards achieving balanced success.

Implementing the **HAF+ Time Report** into my weekly routine provided structure and clarity. By reviewing my past week, identifying hurdles and "aha" moments, identifying the fixes that were put in place to avoid repeating stumbles and setting goals for the upcoming week, I maintained focus and motivation. This practice of regular reflection and planning became integral to my personal and professional growth.

Statistics underscore the urgency of addressing these issues. According to a Gallup poll, only 15% of people worldwide are engaged in their jobs, leaving the majority feeling disconnected and unfulfilled. The American Psychological Association reports that chronic stress is linked to the six leading causes of death, including heart disease, cancer, and suicide. Additionally, research from Harvard Medical School shows that social isolation and loneliness can increase the risk of premature death from all causes, a risk rivaling that of smoking, obesity, and physical inactivity.

These statistics highlight the widespread impact of imbalances in fitness, focus, fraternity, and finance. Without a framework like F4 in place, many individuals risk experiencing similar voids of purpose and fulfillment. By adopting the F4 framework, you can proactively address these challenges, leading to a more balanced, fulfilling, and successful life.

Through this journey, I experienced a profound transformation. I regained my health and energy by incorporating regular exercise and a balanced diet into my routine. I enhanced my focus and productivity by practicing mindfulness and setting clear goals. I rebuilt and strengthened my relationships, finding a sense of community and support that I had been missing. And I achieved financial stability and freedom, not just through my business success, but by adopting smart financial practices and continuous learning.

In this handbook, I will share the principles and practices that have helped me achieve this transformation. The F4 framework is not just a theory; it is a practical, actionable framework to achieving total fulfillment in life. By embracing the principles of Fitness, Focus, Fraternity, and Finance, you too can create a life that is not only successful but deeply satisfying and balanced.

My hope is that this book will inspire you to embark on your own journey of self-discovery and transformation. Whether you are a high achiever seeking to balance your life, a professional looking to enhance your well-being, or anyone in search of greater fulfillment, the **F4 framework** can help you achieve your goals.

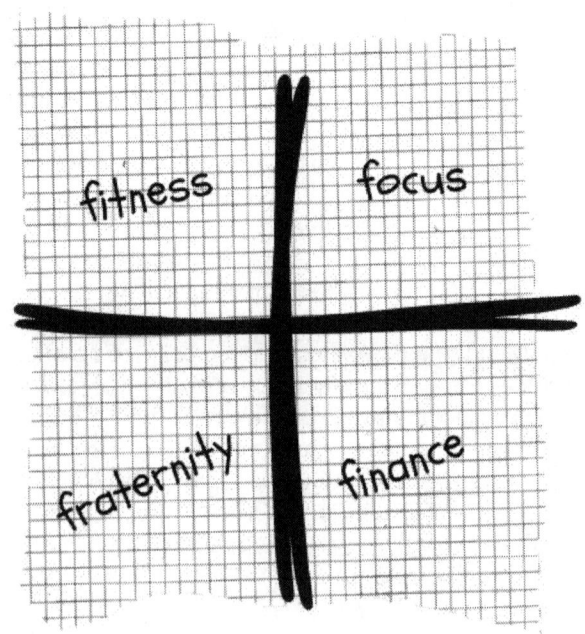

Chapter 1

The Moment of Clarity

"It is not the mountain we conquer but ourselves." – Edmund Hillary

When I sold my company, I thought I had reached the pinnacle of success. Financial stability, the freedom to do whatever I pleased, and the accolades of having built something from the ground up should have brought immense satisfaction. And yet, as I stood at the summit of my achievements, I found myself peering into the abyss of uncertainty.

For years, I had focused intensely on building a successful business. But with that chapter of my life closed, I was suddenly faced with a profound sense of imbalance. Where was I now? And where did I want to go from here? These questions echoed in my mind, louder with each passing day.

It was in this moment of introspection that I realized the importance of clarity. Without a clear understanding of my current situation and a vision for the future, I was like a ship lost at sea, aimlessly drifting without direction. This book accounts the beginning of my journey toward regaining that clarity—assessing where I stood and charting a new course toward a fulfilling life.

The steps that followed were not just about setting goals; they were about understanding the deeper motivations behind those goals, confronting the gaps between my present reality and my desired future, and laying down a path that would lead me to a place of true fulfillment. It was a journey inward as much as it was outward, and it began with the most important question of all:

Where am I now?

Chapter 2

Building Your Vision: Turning Dreams into Action

"Success is the sum of small efforts, repeated day in and day out." - Robert Collier

For as long as I can remember, I've always had big dreams. My mind would race with ideas of what I wanted to achieve, where I wanted to go, and the impact I wanted to make. But for all the energy and excitement those dreams stirred in me, there was one problem—they often remained just that: dreams. They were vivid and inspiring, but they lacked a clear path to turn them into reality.

The Realization: Big Dreams, Small Plans

I'll never forget the moment when I realized that my visions, no matter how grand in my head, were often reduced to much smaller plans when it came time to take action. I would start with a huge goal, but by the time I'd finished mapping out how to achieve it, the plan had shrunk to something far less ambitious.

This was a pattern I saw again and again. I'd start with the intention of making a major change or achieving a lofty goal, but somehow, I'd talk myself down—thinking it was "more realistic" or "more manageable." And while I'd still accomplish things, it was never at the scale I'd originally envisioned.

It was frustrating, to say the least. I knew I was capable of more, but something was holding me back. I needed a new way to approach planning—a way that would allow me to hold onto those big dreams and actually turn them into actionable steps. That's when I developed what I now call the Vision Builder program.

The Birth of Vision Builder: From Dreams to Plans

Vision Builder wasn't something that came to me overnight. It was the result of countless attempts to find a system that worked—something that would allow me to stay true to my big-picture vision while creating a clear path to get there.

The first step was to define where I saw myself right now. I needed to be honest about where I stood in each of the four key areas of my life: Fitness, Focus, Fraternity, and Finance—the pillars I refer to as the F4.

Once I had a clear picture of my current state, I allowed myself to dream big again. I asked myself, "Where do I want to be in the next 12 months?" This was my baseline goal—the one that aligned with the initial vision in my head.

But this time, I didn't stop there.

The Double Vision: Stretching Beyond the Comfort Zone

I knew from experience that simply setting a goal wasn't enough. I needed a way to push myself beyond the limits of what I thought was possible. So, I introduced a concept I call "double vision."

First, I took my 12-month goal and doubled it. I asked myself, "Without worrying about how I'll achieve it, what would it take to get to double this goal?" This became my "adventurous" goal—a target that was both exciting and a little intimidating.

But I didn't stop there. I then took that adventurous goal and doubled it again, creating what I now call my "Reach" goal. This was a goal that felt almost out of reach—something that would truly stretch me and require me to think creatively and act boldly.

Breaking It Down: From Reach to Reality

With my Reach goal in mind, I started to break it down into manageable steps. I knew that trying to achieve such an ambitious goal all at once would be overwhelming, so I asked myself, "What do I need to do in the next three months to be 25% of the way to my Reach goal?" This became my 90-day plan—a focused, achievable target that kept me moving toward the bigger picture.

From there, I broke it down further, asking, "What would it take to be one-third of the way to my 90-day goal by the end of the next month?" This became my 30-day plan—a more immediate set of actions that I could tackle right away.

This process of breaking down the Reach goal into smaller, actionable steps was the key. It allowed me to maintain my focus on the big vision while making tangible progress each day, week, and month.

As I began turning my big dreams into actionable steps, I realized that one of the most crucial aspects of achieving my vision was managing relationships with prospects and clients. Early on, I made the mistake of thinking that success in sales was about pushing hard to close deals. But the more I worked on building my vision, the more I understood that sorting my prospects was far more important than selling to them.

Instead of seeing every interaction as an opportunity to make a sale, I started viewing it as a chance to understand where the prospect was in their journey. Were they just becoming aware of their needs, or were they ready to make a decision? By sorting my prospects into stages—awareness, interest, intent, evaluation, and negotiation—I could tailor my approach to meet them exactly where they were.

This shift in perspective transformed my sales process. I wasn't just closing deals; I was building relationships based on trust and mutual understanding. As a result, my success rate increased, and I found that my clients were more satisfied because they felt understood and supported.

Integrating this approach into my vision-building process allowed me to focus on long-term growth rather than short-term wins. It became a key strategy in achieving the adventurous and reach goals I set for myself, ensuring that every prospect interaction moved me closer to realizing my vision.

The Power of Weekly Planning: Staying on Track

But even with a solid 30-day plan in place, I knew I needed to stay on top of my progress. That's when I integrated the HAF+ Time Report into the Vision Builder program. Each week, I'd reflect on the hurdles I encountered, the "aha" moments I had, and the fixes I implemented. This weekly check-in kept me accountable and allowed me to adjust my course as needed.

By the time the 90-day mark rolled around, even if I hadn't fully reached my most ambitious goals, I was often amazed at how much I had accomplished. I found that by aiming high and breaking down the steps, I was consistently surpassing the original goals I'd set for myself.

The Vision Builder Process: A Practical Guide

Here's how the Vision Builder program works:

Assess Your Current State: Start by being honest about where you are right now in each of the four F4 areas—Fitness, Focus, Fraternity, and Finance.

Pillar	Current State
Fitness	(Your current fitness level)
Focus	(Your current focus level)
Fraternity	(Your current relationships)
Finance	(Your current financial state)

Set Your 12-Month Goal: Define where you want to be in the next 12 months. This is your baseline goal.

Pillar	12-Month Goal
Fitness	(Your fitness goal)
Focus	(Your focus goal)
Fraternity	(Your fraternity goal)
Finance	(Your finance goal)

Apply Double Vision: First, double your 12-month goal to create your "adventurous" goal, then double that to create your "Reach" goal.

Pillar	12-Month	Adventurous	Reach
Fitness	(12-month)	(Double goal)	(Reach)
Focus	(12-month)	(Double goal)	(Reach)
Fraternity	(12-month)	(Double goal)	(Reach)
Finance	(12-month)	(Double goal)	(Reach)

Break It Down: Create your 90-day and 30-day plans by breaking down your Reach goal into smaller steps.

Pillar	Reach Goal	90-Day (25%)	30-Day (1/3)
Fitness	(Reach)	(90-day plan)	(30-day plan)
Focus	(Reach)	(90-day plan)	(30-day plan)
Fraternity	(Reach)	(90-day plan)	(30-day plan)
Finance	(Reach)	(90-day plan)	(30-day plan)

Weekly HAF+ Reports: Use the HAF+ process to stay on track each week, ensuring you're making progress toward your goals.

Pillar	Weekly Goal
Fitness	(Goal for fitness)
Focus	(Goal for focus)
Fraternity	(Goal for relationships)
Finance	(Goal for finances)

The Secret to Success: Aiming Higher, Achieving More

Through the Vision Builder program, I learned that by aiming higher—by pushing myself beyond what seemed reasonable—I could achieve far more than I ever thought possible. The process of breaking down big dreams into actionable steps, while continually reflecting and adjusting, has been the key to turning those dreams into reality.

Even if I don't always hit my Reach goals, I consistently surpass the original goals I set for myself. And in doing so, I've come to realize that the only limits are the ones I place on myself.

Chapter 3

Building Your Plan

A well-structured plan is essential for turning your goals into reality. But for years, I struggled with this. I had the drive, the vision, and the passion, but without a solid plan, my efforts were often scattered and unfocused. It wasn't until I developed a methodical approach to planning that I began to see consistent progress toward my goals. This chapter introduces the **Metric Maker**, a powerful tool designed to help you prioritize and streamline your daily activities, ensuring that you focus on what truly matters.

The Metric Maker: Organizing Your Tasks

The concept of the Metric Maker was born directly from the insights I gained while logging my activities over two days, as discussed in Chapter 2. After meticulously tracking my time and analyzing how I spent my days, I realized that while I was busy, I wasn't always productive. There were clear patterns in how I allocated my time, and I knew I needed a system to help me focus on the activities that would truly drive my success.

The **Metric Maker** is a simple yet effective tool that helps you organize your tasks and projects based on the data from your activity log. It's grounded in the Pareto Principle, which suggests that 80% of your results come from 20% of your efforts. By categorizing your tasks, you can focus on the activities that drive the most value while delegating or eliminating tasks that don't align with your strengths or goals.

Step 1: Listing Your Primary Activities

The first step in using the Metric Maker is to review the activities you logged in Chapter 2. These logged activities provide a clear picture of how you currently spend your time. When I went through this process, I was surprised at the variety of tasks that filled my days. From responding to emails and attending meetings to working on key projects and spending time with family, my days were packed—but not always with high-impact work.

Using the data from your activity log, list all the primary activities you engage in regularly. This list will likely include a mix of professional tasks, personal commitments, and routine responsibilities. By seeing everything laid out in front of you, you can start to identify which activities are consuming your time and which are truly advancing your goals.

Step 2: Delegating Non-Essential Tasks

Once you have your list, the next step is to apply the 80/20 rule. Review the activities you've listed and identify the 80% that are either low-impact or could be delegated to someone else. When I did this, I realized that tasks like scheduling meetings, managing routine communications, and some administrative work were taking up too much of my time. These tasks, while necessary, weren't the ones driving my success.

I decided to delegate these tasks wherever possible. For instance, I handed off scheduling to my assistant and used automation tools to manage routine communications. This freed up a significant portion of my day, allowing me to focus on the 20% of activities that really mattered.

Step 3: Focusing on Core Activities

The final step is to identify the remaining 20% of tasks that are crucial to your success. These are your core activities—the ones that align with your superpowers and contribute most significantly to your goals. For me, these included strategic planning, relationship building with key clients, and content creation, all of which required my unique skills and insights.

By narrowing my focus to these core activities, I found that my productivity soared. I was no longer spread thin across a multitude of tasks. Instead, I concentrated my efforts on the areas where I could have the most impact, and the results were undeniable.

Implementing the Plan

With your tasks now organized into three categories—Primary Activities, Delegate, and Core Activities—you have a clear plan for how to spend your time more effectively. But the Metric Maker isn't just a one-time exercise; it's a dynamic tool that should be revisited regularly. As your responsibilities evolve and new opportunities arise, you need to adjust your task lists to ensure that you're always focusing on the activities that drive the most value.

For me, the Metric Maker became a crucial part of my weekly review process. Every Friday, I would sit down and look over my tasks from the past week, assessing where I had spent my time and where I could improve. This habit of regular reflection and adjustment kept me aligned with my goals and helped me stay focused on what really mattered.

The Impact of a Well-Structured Plan

The transformation in my productivity and overall satisfaction was profound. By focusing on the activities that aligned with my core values and strengths, I was able to make significant strides toward my goals. The stress of juggling countless tasks began to fade, replaced by a sense of purpose and clarity.

The Metric Maker didn't just help me get organized; it helped me prioritize my life. It allowed me to ensure that every action I took was leading me closer to the life I wanted to build. And that's the real power of a well-structured plan—it gives you the confidence to move forward, knowing that your efforts are aligned with your most important goals.

The next chapter will introduce the importance of logging your activities, enabling you to track your efforts and maintain alignment with your goals. But for now, remember that the key to success is not just hard work; it's smart work. And smart work starts with a clear, focused plan.

Chapter 4

Logging Your Activity

Success begins with awareness, and awareness starts with understanding how you spend your time. This chapter focuses on the foundational practice of logging your daily activities, a critical first step in optimizing your productivity and aligning your actions with your long-term goals.

The Power of Activity Logging

For years, I operated on autopilot, moving from one task to the next without fully recognizing where my time was going. It wasn't until I took a step back and began logging my activities that I realized how much time was slipping through the cracks. This lack of awareness was leading to inefficiencies and a persistent feeling of being overwhelmed.

When I first started logging my activities, I didn't expect it to be as revealing as it was. By meticulously tracking my time over the course of two days, I began to see patterns—moments where I was productive and times when I was merely spinning my wheels. This exercise brought unconscious behaviors to light, enabling me to make informed decisions about where to focus my efforts.

The Two-Day Activity Log

To get a clear picture of how you spend your time, I recommend logging your activities over two consecutive days. This practice involves recording your start time, the activity you engaged in, and the end time for each task. Be honest and detailed—every activity, no matter how small, should be logged.

Here's an example of what your activity log might look like:

Time	Activity	Duration
7:00 AM	Morning workout	1 hour
8:30 AM	Checking and responding to emails	1 hour
9:30 AM	Team meeting	1 hour
10:30 AM	Project work (focused)	2 hours
12:30 PM	Lunch	1 hour
1:30 PM	Client calls	1.5 hours
3:00 PM	Break/Walk	30 minutes
3:30 PM	Continued project work	2 hours
5:30 PM	End of workday review and planning	30 minutes
8:00 PM	Leisure/Reading	1 hour

When I first did this exercise, I was surprised by how much time I spent on low-value activities. It was eye-opening to see the amount of time I dedicated to tasks that didn't contribute to my long-term goals. By capturing this data over two days, I was able to account for variability in my schedule and get a balanced view of how I was truly spending my time.

Analyzing Your Time

Once you've completed your activity logs, it's essential to review and analyze the data. As I looked over my logs, patterns began to emerge. I noticed that certain activities consistently took up more time than they should, while others were squeezed into short, unfocused bursts.

This analysis helped me identify where I was wasting time and where I could be more productive. For instance, I realized that I was spending too much time on emails and meetings that could have been streamlined or delegated. By understanding where my time was going, I was able to make strategic decisions about how to allocate my most valuable resource—my time.

Taking Control of Your Day

The simple act of logging my activities gave me a new sense of control over my day. I was no longer at the mercy of distractions or inefficient habits. Instead, I could consciously choose where to focus my energy. This was the first step in transforming my approach to time management and productivity.

Logging your activities may seem tedious at first, but the insights you gain are invaluable. It's about more than just tracking time—it's about gaining the awareness needed to make meaningful changes in your life. By taking this step, you set yourself up for greater success and alignment with your long-term goals.

Chapter 5

The System – The Central Hub

A well-organized system is the backbone of efficient task management and clear communication. In this chapter, we introduce the Central Hub, a unified project and task capturing system that centralizes all your responsibilities in one place.

The Central Hub: Organizing Tasks and Projects

The concept of the Central Hub was born out of necessity, but I'll be honest—it didn't start out smoothly. When I first tried to implement this system, it felt like more trouble than it was worth. I was used to handling things myself, often thinking, "I can do this faster than explaining it to someone else." Trying to organize tasks, delegate them properly, and ensure everything was documented seemed like it would slow me down, not speed me up.

But over time, as I kept pushing myself to use the Central Hub, something shifted. I began to see the benefits of having everything in one place, clearly organized and accessible to everyone who needed it. The initial frustration gave way to a realization: this was a far better way to operate.

As I started organizing tasks and projects within the Central Hub, I quickly realized that knowing what to do was only half the battle. The other half was actually getting those tasks done, especially when focus was in short supply. That's when I discovered the Pomodoro Technique—a simple yet powerful method to boost productivity by breaking work into manageable intervals.

The Pomodoro Technique involves working in focused bursts of 25 minutes, followed by a 5-minute break. After four of these cycles, you take a longer break of 15 to 30 minutes. I found this method particularly effective for staying on task, especially when dealing with complex projects that could easily become overwhelming.

I began integrating Pomodoro sessions into my daily routine, using them to tackle high-priority tasks within the Central Hub. The technique not only helped me stay focused but also made daunting projects feel more manageable by breaking them down into smaller, timed segments. It was a game-changer for my productivity, allowing me to maintain a rhythm of deep work throughout the day.

By combining the organizational power of the Central Hub with the Pomodoro Technique, I was able to maintain a high level of productivity while avoiding burnout. This combination became a cornerstone of my approach to task management, ensuring that I stayed on track without losing focus.

The **Central Hub** became more than just a project management tool; it turned into the command center for my life and work. It brought together all the pieces—tasks, projects, deadlines, and communication—into one cohesive system. Each task or project within the Central Hub includes:

- **One Owner:** Every task or project is assigned to a single owner who is responsible for its completion, ensuring accountability.
- **Task/Project Description:** A detailed description of the task or project outlines what needs to be done, providing clarity and direction.
- **Due Date:** Each task is assigned a due date, prioritizing tasks and ensuring that projects move forward on schedule.
- **Level of Delegation:** The level of delegation (Manage, Lead, Empower) is specified, clarifying the degree of autonomy the task owner has.
- **File Links:** A column is dedicated to linking necessary files required to complete the task, ensuring that resources are easily accessible.
- **Training Videos:** Another column is reserved for links to training videos or tutorials that might be helpful for completing the task effectively.

Once I fully committed to using the Central Hub, I realized how much time I was actually saving. Instead of constantly putting out fires and juggling tasks in my head, I had a clear, organized system that allowed me to manage everything more efficiently. What once felt like an extra burden became the backbone of my productivity.

Asynchronous Communication: Keeping Teams Aligned

One of the biggest challenges I faced in managing projects and tasks was the constant barrage of communication—emails, messages, phone calls—all demanding immediate attention. It was distracting and disruptive, pulling me away from deep work and critical thinking. To address this, I integrated an asynchronous communication policy into the Central Hub.

Asynchronous communication allows team members to send and receive information without the expectation of an immediate response. This reduces interruptions and allows everyone to maintain focus during their work. It also ensures that important information is documented and accessible, rather than being lost in a flurry of real-time conversations.

Key components of asynchronous communication in the Central Hub include:

- **Voice Communication:** Utilize voice messages or recorded audio notes for conveying tone and nuance that text may lack. This is especially useful for complex instructions or sensitive topics.
- **Text Communication:** Text-based communication, such as email or messaging apps, provides a written record of conversations and is ideal for sharing information that can be referenced later.
- **Video Communication:** Video messages or recorded video updates can convey more detailed instructions or provide visual context for tasks. These are particularly helpful when explaining complex concepts or when a face-to-face meeting isn't possible.

At first, adjusting to asynchronous communication felt like another obstacle. I was used to the immediacy of real-time conversations. But as I leaned into the process, I noticed how much it reduced distractions and improved the quality of my work. It allowed me to maintain focus on deep work while still keeping the team aligned and informed.

Integrating the System

The Central Hub and asynchronous communication policy work together to create a cohesive system that supports efficient task management and effective communication. By centralizing all project and task information in the Central Hub, you ensure that everyone has access to the resources and instructions they need. Meanwhile, the asynchronous communication policy keeps teams connected and informed without sacrificing focus.

The more I used this system, the more I saw its value. What started as a frustrating change turned into a powerful tool that kept everything on track. I no longer had to juggle a thousand things in my mind; instead, I could rely on the Central Hub to manage the details, freeing up my mental energy for more strategic thinking.

The Power of a Centralized System

The Central Hub didn't just improve my productivity; it gave me peace of mind. I knew that everything was in its place, that tasks were progressing as they should, and that communication was clear and effective. This system became the foundation upon which I built my success.

But like any system, the Central Hub is not static. It evolves as your needs and responsibilities change. Regularly review and refine your system to ensure it continues to serve you well. As new projects and tasks come into play, adapt your Central Hub to accommodate them, keeping everything organized and manageable.

In the next chapter, we'll delve into the art of alignment,

helping you harmonize your daily tasks with your overarching vision. But for now, remember that the key to staying on top of your game is not just about working harder; it's about working smarter, with a system that supports your success.

Chapter 6

The Art of Alignment

Balance. It's a word we hear often, yet it can feel elusive, especially when we're striving to achieve big goals. For years, I believed that if I just worked hard enough, put in enough hours, and pushed myself to the limit, I could accomplish anything. But that mindset came at a cost. I was burning out, losing touch with the things that mattered most, and feeling increasingly disconnected from the very life I was trying to build.

It wasn't until I understood the importance of alignment—ensuring that all aspects of my life were in harmony—that I began to truly experience balance. This chapter explores how to achieve that balance, not by working harder, but by aligning your life with your values, goals, and priorities.

The Myth of Work-Life Balance

The concept of work-life balance is often presented as a scale that needs to be perfectly balanced at all times. But life isn't that simple. There are times when work demands more of your energy, and other times when personal life takes precedence. The key isn't in trying to achieve a perfect 50/50 balance; it's in creating a dynamic alignment that allows you to thrive in both areas.

I remember a time when I was so focused on my work that I neglected everything else. I was successful in my career, but at what cost? My relationships were strained, my health was suffering, and I felt disconnected from the things that once brought me joy. It was a wake-up call that made me realize I needed to change my approach.

I began to see balance not as a static state but as a dynamic process of alignment. It's about making conscious choices that reflect your values and priorities in the moment. Some days, that means dedicating more time to work, while other days, it means prioritizing family, health, or personal growth. The goal is to create a life where all the pieces fit together in a way that feels right for you.

The Four Pillars of Alignment

To achieve balance, I developed a framework based on what I call the **Four Pillars of Alignment**: **Fitness**, **Focus**, **Fraternity**, and **Finance**. These pillars represent the core areas of life that need to be in harmony for you to feel balanced and fulfilled.

1. **Fitness**: This pillar represents your physical health and well-being. It's about taking care of your body through exercise, nutrition, and rest. When I was out of balance, fitness was often the first thing to go. I would skip workouts, eat poorly, and ignore the signs that my body was struggling. But I learned that without physical health, everything else suffers. Prioritizing fitness became a non-negotiable part of my daily routine.
2. **Focus**: This pillar is about mental clarity and productivity. It's ensuring that your mind is sharp and that you're working on the right things. When I was overwhelmed, my focus was scattered. I would jump from task to task without a clear plan, leading to inefficiency and frustration. By prioritizing focus, I was able to

streamline my efforts and achieve more with less stress.
3. **Fraternity**: This pillar represents your relationships and connections with others. It's about nurturing the bonds that matter most to you—family, friends, colleagues, and community. During my most unbalanced times, my relationships suffered. I was so consumed with work that I neglected the people who mattered most. Reconnecting with them and making time for meaningful interactions became a priority, and it made all the difference in my overall sense of fulfillment.
4. **Finance**: This pillar is about financial health and security. It's ensuring that your financial situation supports your goals and allows you to live the life you want. There were times when I was so focused on earning more that I lost sight of why I was doing it. Financial goals are important, but they need to be aligned with your values and overall vision for your life. When I started viewing finance as a means to support my broader goals rather than an end in itself, I found a much healthier balance.

Creating Your Alignment Plan

Achieving balance starts with assessing where you are in each of these four pillars. I developed a simple exercise that helped me—and can help you—get clear on what needs attention. For each pillar, ask yourself the following questions:

1. **Where am I now?**
2. **Where do I want to be?**
3. **What actions do I need to take to get there?**

When I first did this exercise, the gaps were glaring. I

realized that while I was excelling in my career (Finance), my Fitness and Fraternity pillars were severely neglected. This awareness allowed me to create a plan that prioritized the areas that needed the most attention, while still maintaining progress in the areas where I was already strong.

The Art of Dynamic Alignment

The reality is that balance is never perfect—it's constantly shifting. There will be times when one pillar needs more attention than the others, and that's okay. The goal is not to achieve perfect equilibrium but to be aware of the imbalances and make conscious adjustments.

One of the most powerful lessons I learned was to regularly check in with myself. I made it a habit to review my alignment plan weekly, assessing where I was and making any necessary adjustments. This simple practice allowed me to stay connected to my values and priorities, ensuring that I was living a life that felt aligned and fulfilling.

Living a Balanced Life

Achieving balance is an ongoing journey, not a destination. It requires self-awareness, flexibility, and a commitment to living in alignment with your values. When all the pieces of your life are working together, you'll find that you're not only more successful but also more content, energized, and fulfilled.

In the next chapter, we'll explore how to unleash your superpowers, enabling you to maximize your potential and achieve greater results. But for now, remember that balance is not about perfection; it's about alignment, and alignment is within your reach.

Chapter 7

Unleashing Your Superpowers

Your core values and strengths are the engines that drive your success. Unleashing them begins with understanding what truly energizes you—what I call your "superpowers." This chapter dives into the process of discovering those superpowers and using that knowledge to focus your efforts where you can make the most impact.

Identifying Your Core Values

Several years ago, I found myself feeling drained, despite the success I had achieved. I realized that much of my energy was being spent on activities that didn't align with my core values. This misalignment was a silent drain on my motivation and well-being. To reclaim my energy, I needed to clarify what I truly valued—those principles that would guide my decisions and actions moving forward.

To start this process, I reflected on a list of 12 powerful words, each representing a potential core value:

1. **Reliability**
2. **Consistency**
3. **Efficiency**
4. **Innovation**

5. **Creativity**
6. **Motivation**
7. **Optimism**
8. **Passion**
9. **Fitness**
10. **Perseverance**
11. **Service**
12. **Resilience**

These words weren't just arbitrary choices; they were reflections of what drove me and what gave me energy. I took the time to consider each word carefully, asking myself which of these values genuinely resonated with me, inspired me, and aligned with the person I wanted to be.

In the end, I selected three that stood out most: **Innovation, Perseverance, and Service**. These values became my guiding principles, helping me navigate decisions and focus my energy on what truly mattered.

This exercise was a turning point. By identifying my core values, I was able to align my daily actions with what truly mattered to me. It was like finding a compass that pointed me in the right direction, every time.

Assessing Your Strengths and Weaknesses

With my core values in hand, the next step was to take an honest look at my strengths and weaknesses. This wasn't an easy process. Admitting where I excelled was as challenging as acknowledging where I fell short. But this self-assessment was crucial for understanding where I should focus my energy and where I might need support.

I asked myself three open-ended questions:

1. **I am awesome at...**
2. **I am decent at...**
3. **I am awful at...**

At first, I hesitated to fill in the blanks. It's hard to admit weaknesses, and sometimes even harder to recognize your strengths. But the more honest I was with myself, the clearer the picture became. I discovered that I thrived when I was engaging in activities that aligned with my core values. These were my superpower activities—tasks that not only energized me but also allowed me to make the greatest impact.

On the flip side, I realized that there were areas where I was just decent or downright awful. These were tasks that drained me, where my efforts were better spent finding someone else to handle them or learning how to improve.

Discovering Your Superpower Activities

As I dug deeper, I began to identify the core activities that made me feel alive and in tune with my values. These were the tasks that, when I engaged in them, time seemed to fly by. I was in a state of flow—fully immersed and thriving.

For example, I found that mentoring others was one

of my superpower activities. Whether it was guiding a colleague through a tough decision or helping someone develop a new skill, these moments brought out the best in me. They didn't just align with my values of **Service** and **Perseverance**—they energized me in ways that other tasks simply couldn't.

Once I identified these superpower activities, I made a conscious effort to focus more of my time and energy on them. This wasn't about ignoring the tasks I wasn't great at—it was about maximizing the impact of what I was already naturally inclined to do well.

Self-Assessment: Where You Are Now?

With a better understanding of my core values and strengths, I took a moment to reflect on my current situation. I asked myself three simple but powerful questions:

1. **I am...** (This is my current identity.)
2. **I want to...** (These are my desires for the future.)
3. **I have to...** (These are the obligations I feel are necessary to achieve my goals.)

These questions weren't just for reflection—they were for action. They helped me articulate where I was and where I wanted to go. By aligning my superpowers with my goals, I was able to create a path forward that was not only achievable but also deeply fulfilling.

Unleashing Your Superpowers

The journey of identifying and unleashing your superpowers is transformative. It's about understanding who you are at your core, recognizing what energizes you, and focusing your efforts where they can make the most impact. When you operate from this place of strength and alignment, you'll find that success comes more naturally, and with it, a profound sense of fulfillment.

In the next chapter, we'll focus on how to delegate activities effectively, freeing up your time and energy for the most impactful tasks. But remember, the foundation of that plan starts here—with a deep understanding of what makes you, you.

Chapter 8

How to Delegate Activities

Delegation is a skill that, when mastered, can significantly enhance your productivity and the effectiveness of your team. In this chapter, we explore the art of delegation, focusing on the three levels of delegation: Manage, Lead, and Empower.

The Essence of Delegation

Delegation is not about letting go, but about strategically deploying the best resources with clarity to get tasks done efficiently. Effective delegation allows you to conserve your energy for the activities that truly matter while empowering others to contribute their best. It's about maximizing efficiency with the least amount of your energy expended.

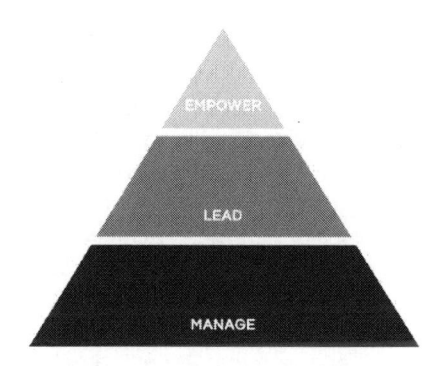

I used to think of delegation as simply handing off tasks I didn't want to do. But I soon realized that delegation is much more nuanced. It's about understanding the strengths of your team members and assigning tasks that align with those strengths. It's about trusting others to take ownership and allowing them the space to make decisions and grow.

The Three Levels of Delegation

Through trial and error, I discovered that not all tasks can be delegated in the same way. Some require close supervision, while others can be handed off entirely. This understanding led me to develop a framework I call the **Three Levels of Delegation**: **Manage, Lead, and Empower**.

Manage

At the **Manage** level, you are closely involved in the task being delegated. You manage all the decisions that need to be made to complete the task, providing explicit instructions on how it should be done. The person carrying out the task understands that they are to follow your instructions precisely, and if any decision points arise, they are expected to consult you.

I first encountered the need for this level of delegation when working on a critical project that required precision and attention to detail. The stakes were high, and I couldn't afford any mistakes. I assigned the task to a team member who was relatively new, knowing that they needed close guidance. By managing the task closely, I ensured that the outcome met the high standards required.

Lead
When delegating at the **Lead** level, you begin to transfer some decision-making responsibility to the person handling the task. The individual is expected to take initiative by:

- Providing three solutions to complete the task.
- Labeling each solution as **good**, **better**, or **best**.
- Reviewing their solutions with you and explaining the reasoning behind each ranking.

After reviewing the options, you'll decide which solution to proceed with and explain why that choice is the best. This level of delegation allows the person to take on more responsibility while still benefiting from your guidance.

I remember a time when I needed to delegate the creation of a marketing campaign. I wanted to encourage creativity while still maintaining some control over the direction. By using the **Lead** level of delegation, I allowed my team member to explore different ideas, present them, and learn through the process of evaluating the best approach together. This not only improved the outcome but also helped my team member develop confidence in their decision-making skills.

Empower
Empowerment is the highest level of delegation, where you fully trust the person to make all the decisions needed to complete the task. At this stage, you empower them to take ownership of the task, including any decisions that arise during its execution.

Your role shifts from being a decision-maker to

being a supporter. You promise to fully back the person in the decisions they make, providing them with the autonomy they need to achieve the desired outcome.

I first learned to fully empower a team member when I was overwhelmed with multiple projects. I assigned a crucial task to a senior colleague, someone I knew was capable and experienced. I handed them the reins and let them take full control. The result was not only a successful project but also a stronger, more motivated team member who felt valued and trusted.

The Goal of Delegation

The ultimate goal of delegation is to move your team members toward the **Empower** stage, where they can independently handle tasks with the same level of excellence and attention to detail that you would expect from yourself. This approach not only enhances your productivity but also cultivates a more capable and confident team.

Through effective delegation, I was able to free up my time to focus on the core activities that required my unique strengths. I also noticed that my team members were more engaged and motivated, as they were given opportunities to grow and contribute meaningfully to the success of our projects.

Overcoming the Fear of Letting Go

One of the biggest challenges I faced with delegation was the fear of letting go. I worried that tasks wouldn't be done to my standards or that mistakes would be made. But what I learned is that mistakes are part of the process. They provide valuable learning opportunities for both the person completing the task and for me as a leader.

By letting go, I not only increased my productivity but also empowered my team to step up, take ownership, and grow in their roles. The sense of trust that delegation fosters is invaluable in building a strong, cohesive team.

Delegation as a Strategic Tool

Delegation is not just a way to offload work; it's a strategic tool for growth—both for you and your team. It allows you to focus on what you do best while developing the skills and capabilities of those around you. As you become more comfortable with delegation, you'll find that your capacity to lead and achieve your goals expands.

In the next chapter, we'll discuss how prioritizing fitness can enhance your productivity and overall well-being. But for now, remember that delegation is not about losing control; it's about empowering others and building a stronger, more efficient team.

Chapter 9

Success Begins with Fitness

"The greatest wealth is health." - Virgil

Success in any area of life requires a strong foundation, and that foundation begins with fitness. For years, I underestimated the role that physical health played in my overall success. I thought that as long as I was working hard and putting in the hours, I could power through anything. But eventually, the lack of attention to my physical well-being caught up with me. I was burning out, struggling to focus, and finding it harder to sustain the energy I needed to reach my goals. That's when I realized that fitness wasn't just a nice-to-have—it was essential.

Fitness as the Cornerstone of Success

Fitness is often seen as something separate from our professional and personal goals, but the truth is, it's the cornerstone upon which all other successes are built. When your body is strong and healthy, your mind is clearer, your energy levels are higher, and you're better equipped to handle the challenges that come your way.

I remember a time when I was so focused on work that I completely neglected my health. I skipped workouts, ate whatever was convenient, and got by on too little sleep. At first, it seemed like I was saving time, but soon I began to notice the effects. My productivity plummeted, I was constantly fatigued, and my mood was often sour. It became clear that without a strong foundation of fitness, everything else was starting to crumble.

That's when I made a commitment to prioritize my

health, not as an afterthought, but as a central part of my routine. And at the core of this commitment was a simple but powerful principle: **"Show Up."**

While committing to my fitness routine was a crucial first step, I soon realized that maintaining balance across all four pillars of the F4 Framework required more than just a good start—it needed consistency. But life is unpredictable, and there were weeks when hitting all my goals felt impossible. That's when I developed the F4 Fallback—a set of base goals that I could rely on no matter how busy or chaotic things got.

These fallback goals were simple but effective. For fitness, I committed to sweating for at least 15 minutes each day, even if that just meant a brisk walk. For focus,

I set aside 5 minutes for meditation, giving my mind the space it needed to reset. Fraternity involved reaching out to five contacts each week to maintain and nurture my relationships. And finally, for finance, I made sure to do one activity that would move my wealth or career forward, whether it was reviewing my budget, making a new connection, or learning a new skill.

These goals weren't meant to be ambitious—they were my safety net. On weeks when everything went according to plan, I often exceeded these goals. But on the tough weeks, when nothing seemed to go right, these fallback goals ensured that I still made progress. They became the foundation of my consistency, helping me stay on track even when life threw me off balance.

Just Show Up

When it comes to fitness, sometimes just showing up is all you need to do. Early on, I learned that setting overly ambitious goals or trying to do too much too soon was a recipe for burnout. The key to building a lasting fitness habit was to start small and focus on consistency. Even on days when I didn't feel like working out, I made it a point to show up—whether that meant lacing up my running shoes, getting to the gym, or rolling out my yoga mat.

At first, I told myself, "Just show up." I didn't put pressure on myself to have the best workout or to push my limits every time. Some days, I would do a light workout, while on others, I would find the energy to push harder once I got started. But the important thing was that I kept showing up, even when I didn't feel like it.

By committing to this principle, I avoided the trap of giving up when I felt like, well, giving up. Showing up became a non-negotiable part of my routine. It wasn't about perfection; it was about persistence. And over time, that persistence paid off in ways I hadn't anticipated.

Building a Fitness Routine

Creating a fitness routine that supports your goals doesn't have to be complicated. It's about consistency and making choices that align with your lifestyle. Here's how I approached it:

1. **Start Small, Build Consistency**: When I first got back into fitness, I didn't try to overhaul my life overnight. I started with small, manageable steps—short morning workouts, a focus on drinking more water, and getting to bed a little earlier. These small changes, when done consistently, began to add up, and over time, they became habits. The key was to show up every day, no matter how small the effort seemed.
2. **Choose Activities You Enjoy**: Fitness doesn't have to mean spending hours in the gym doing exercises you hate. I found that the key to sticking with a routine was choosing activities I enjoyed. Whether it was a brisk walk, a bike ride, or a yoga session, the important thing was that I looked forward to it. This made it easier to stay consistent and integrate fitness into my daily life. And even when I wasn't in the mood, I reminded myself to just show up.
3. **Prioritize Recovery and Rest**: In the beginning, I made the mistake of thinking that more was always better. I would push myself to the point of exhaustion, believing that it was the only way to see results. But I quickly learned that recovery and rest are just as important as the workouts themselves. I started listening to my body, giving myself time to recover, and ensuring I was

getting enough sleep. This approach not only improved my fitness but also helped me avoid burnout. Even on rest days, I stayed committed to the principle of showing up by doing something active, like a gentle stretch or a short walk.

The Ripple Effect of Fitness

As my fitness improved, I began to notice a ripple effect across all areas of my life. My energy levels soared, my focus sharpened, and I found it easier to stay disciplined in my work. The confidence I gained from taking care of my body translated into greater confidence in my professional endeavors.

One of the most surprising benefits was the impact on my mental health. Regular exercise became a way to manage stress, clear my mind, and boost my mood. It provided me with a sense of control and accomplishment, which spilled over into everything else I did.

Fitness became more than just a physical pursuit—it became a key part of my success strategy. By investing in my health and consistently showing up, I was investing in my future, and the returns were undeniable.

Fitness as a Non-Negotiable

Today, fitness is a non-negotiable part of my routine. It's not something I squeeze in when I have time; it's something I prioritize because I know it's the foundation for everything else I want to achieve. Whether it's a morning workout to start the day on the right foot or a stretch session to wind down, I make sure that fitness remains a central focus. And no matter how busy or unmotivated I might feel, I always remember to just show up.

I've also learned to be flexible with my approach. There are times when work or travel makes it difficult to stick to my usual routine, but instead of letting it slide, I adapt. I find ways to stay active, even if it means a quick workout in a hotel room or a walk between meetings. The key is to keep moving, no matter what.

Fitness and Long-Term Success

The benefits of fitness extend far beyond the immediate. By prioritizing your physical health and committing to the simple act of showing up, you're setting yourself up for long-term success. You're building the stamina, resilience, and mental clarity needed to tackle big challenges and pursue your goals with determination.

In the next chapter, we'll explore the role of focus in achieving success and how honing your ability to concentrate can take your efforts to the next level. But for now, remember that success begins with fitness. By taking care of your body and showing up consistently, you're laying the groundwork for everything else you want to achieve.

Chapter 10

Focus - The Discipline of Taking Time

"The successful warrior is the average man, with laser-like focus." - Bruce Lee

In our fast-paced world, the idea of slowing down to focus can seem counterintuitive. We're constantly bombarded with information, tasks, and responsibilities that demand our attention. But if there's one thing I've learned on my journey to success, it's this: to be more intentional, strategic, and joyful, you've got to make time for yourself. This isn't just about being more productive; it's about creating space to think, reflect, and connect with what truly matters.

The Many Faces of Focus Time

I know that people see this in different ways. Some call it reading time, others refer to it as meditation, chair time, prayer, stretching, or simply taking a moment to breathe. The labels vary, but the essence is the same—the goal is to carve out time to quiet your mind, disconnect from the noise, and reconnect with yourself.

For me, this time has taken many forms over the years. Sometimes it's a quiet morning spent reading a book that inspires me. Other times, it's a few minutes of meditation to center myself before a busy day. There have been days when a simple stretch routine does the trick, allowing me to feel my body and clear my mind. And of course, there are moments of prayer, where I seek guidance and express gratitude.

Whatever you choose to call it, the bottom line is that taking this time is crucial if you want to be more intentional about your life and work. It's not about following a specific method or ritual; it's about finding what works for you and making it a regular part of your routine.

The Power of Stillness

When I first started incorporating this practice into my life, it felt strange. I was so used to being in constant motion—working, solving problems, moving from one task to the next—that the idea of sitting still and doing "nothing" seemed almost wasteful. But as I leaned into it, I began to realize the power of stillness.

Taking time to be still, whether it's through meditation, prayer, or simply sitting in silence, allows you to step back from the whirlwind of daily life. It gives you a chance to observe your thoughts without judgment, to feel your emotions without being overwhelmed by them, and to gain clarity on what truly matters.

This time of stillness became a sanctuary for me—a place where I could reconnect with my purpose and align my actions with my values. It wasn't just about relaxing; it was about creating space for strategic thinking, for envisioning the future I wanted to build, and for ensuring that my day-to-day actions were aligned with my long-term goals.

Creating Your Focus Routine

Building a focus routine doesn't have to be complicated. It's about making time, even if it's just a few minutes each day, to step away from the chaos and center yourself. Here's how I approached it:

1. **Start Small**: You don't need to carve out hours of your day to reap the benefits of focus time. Start with just five or ten minutes. Whether it's first thing in the morning, during a lunch break, or before bed, find a time that works for you and commit to it.
2. **Find What Resonates with You**: There's no one-size-fits-all approach to focus time. Experiment with different practices—reading, meditation, prayer, stretching—and see what resonates with you. The key is to find something that helps you disconnect from the external noise and reconnect with yourself.
3. **Make It a Non-Negotiable**: Life gets busy, and it's easy to let this time slip through the cracks. But if you want to be more intentional and strategic, you need to make focus time a non-negotiable part of your routine. Treat it with the same importance as any other meeting or task on your to-do list.
4. **Allow Yourself to Just Be**: Focus time isn't about achieving anything in particular; it's about allowing yourself to just be. Don't pressure yourself to have profound insights or solve all your problems in these moments. Simply give yourself permission to exist in the present, to feel your feelings, and to let your thoughts flow freely.

The Impact of Focus Time

As I made focus time a regular part of my life, I began to notice profound changes. I became more intentional in my decisions, more strategic in my planning, and more joyful in my day-to-day life. The clarity and calm I gained from these moments allowed me to approach challenges with a fresh perspective and renewed energy.

Focus time helped me to see the bigger picture, to align my actions with my values, and to ensure that I was moving in the direction I truly wanted to go. It became a cornerstone of my success, not because it made me more productive, but because it made me more connected to what really mattered.

Make Time, Reap the Rewards

The practice of taking time for yourself is one of the most powerful tools you can use to create a life of intention, strategy, and joy. It's not about the label you give it or the method you choose; it's about making the time. By committing to this practice, you're giving yourself the gift of clarity, focus, and inner peace—qualities that are essential for achieving success on your terms.

In the next chapter, we'll explore how to bring all these elements together—fitness, focus, strategy, and joy—into a cohesive plan for living a fulfilling and successful life. But for now, remember that the journey begins with a simple commitment: to make time for yourself, every day, in whatever way resonates with you.

Chapter 11

The Importance of Fraternity

"Friendship is born at that moment when one person says to another, 'What! You too? I thought I was the only one.'" - C.S. Lewis

Success is built on the foundation of strong relationships. The people we connect with, the communities we engage in, and the networks we cultivate are critical to our personal and professional growth. But there's a limit to how many relationships we can effectively manage. Research and experience have shown that most people can only maintain meaningful relationships with about 150 contacts at any given time. This concept, known as "Dunbar's Number," highlights the cognitive and emotional limits of our social networks. But how do you manage these 150 relationships effectively? That's where the Relate Matrix comes in.

As I deepened my understanding of relationships through the Relate Matrix, I realized that this approach could be applied to the sales process as well. Just as I categorized my personal and professional relationships based on depth and transparency, I began to think about my prospects in a similar way. What if, instead of trying to sell to every prospect the same way, I managed the sales process from their perspective?

This led me to adopt a new approach: guiding prospects through five key stages—awareness, interest, intent, evaluation, and negotiation. At each stage, my role wasn't to push for a sale but to provide the right information and support based on where the prospect was in their decision-making process.

For instance, when a prospect was in the awareness stage, I focused on educating them about their needs and the solutions available. As they moved into the interest stage, I provided more detailed information about how my offerings could meet those needs. By the time they reached the intent and evaluation stages, we were discussing specific benefits and addressing any concerns they had.

This perspective shift not only made the sales process smoother but also strengthened my relationships with clients. They appreciated that I wasn't just trying to close a deal—I was genuinely interested in helping them make the best decision. This approach aligned perfectly with the principles of fraternity, fostering trust and long-term partnerships.

Why 150 Contacts? Understanding the Limitations

The idea that we can only manage around 150 meaningful relationships stems from anthropological research, particularly the work of British anthropologist Robin Dunbar. Dunbar's studies suggested that this number is a result of cognitive constraints—our brains are only capable of maintaining a certain number of stable social relationships. These aren't just casual acquaintances; they're people with whom you can maintain close ties, keep up with their lives, and interact regularly.

In my own experience, I found this concept to be true. Despite my best efforts, I realized there was a limit to the number of relationships I could maintain at a meaningful level. This led me to develop a structured approach to managing relationships—a model that would allow me to prioritize and deepen connections effectively. This approach became the Relate Matrix.

The Creation of the Relate Matrix

The Relate Matrix was designed to help manage relationships by categorizing them based on two key dimensions: **Depth of Relationship** and **Transparency of Interaction**. Understanding and mapping these dimensions are essential for managing and deepening relationships effectively.

1. **Y-Axis: Depth of Relationship**
   The y-axis of the Relate Matrix represents the depth of your relationship with a contact. This depth is divided into five stages, reflecting how close and meaningful the relationship is:
   - **Stranger**: At the lowest level, these are people you've met but have not established any significant connection with. Interaction is minimal and often superficial.
   - **Acquaintance**: These are individuals you know by name and face, with whom you have casual interactions. There's some recognition, but the relationship hasn't developed much beyond that.
   - **Casual Friend**: These are people you interact with somewhat regularly. There's a basic level of trust and comfort, but the relationship remains on the surface.
   - **Close Friend**: At this stage, the relationship has deepened significantly. There is mutual trust, understanding, and regular interaction. You can rely on each other in meaningful ways.
   - **Intimate Friend**: This is the highest

level of relationship depth. Intimate friends are those with whom you share your most personal thoughts, feelings, and experiences. These relationships are built on a foundation of deep trust, vulnerability, and consistent support.

2. **X-Axis: Transparency of Interaction**
   The x-axis of the Relate Matrix represents the transparency of your interactions with a contact. This transparency is divided into three stages, reflecting how open and honest you are in your communications:
   - **Skill-Based**: At this level, interactions are primarily transactional or professional. You engage with the person based on specific skills or tasks, without sharing much personal information.
   - **Conditional Transparency**: This stage involves sharing more personal information, but with certain boundaries. You're open to a degree, but you still maintain some level of reservation, depending on the context of the relationship.
   - **Fully Transparent**: At this highest level, you interact with complete openness and honesty. You share your true thoughts, feelings, and experiences without holding back. This level of transparency typically coincides with the deepest relationships.

Each contact is plotted on the Relate Matrix based on where they fall along these two dimensions. This visual representation provides a clear picture of your relationship landscape, allowing you to see which relationships are thriving and which may need more attention.

Using the Relate Matrix to Value Contacts

The Relate Matrix isn't just about categorizing your relationships—it's a tool to help you value and manage them effectively. By understanding where each contact falls on the matrix, you can determine how much value they bring to your life and how much effort you should invest in maintaining or deepening the relationship.

1. **Seasonal vs. Franchise Contacts**:
    - **Seasonal Contacts**: These are relationships that are important during specific phases of your life or work. They may be more relevant at certain times but are not necessarily long-term connections. Understanding the seasonal nature of these relationships allows you to adjust your efforts accordingly, focusing on them when they're most relevant and letting them fade when they're not.
    - **Franchise Contacts**: These are the cornerstone relationships in your life—those that remain significant over time and require consistent nurturing. Franchise contacts are those with whom you share deep bonds, and they should be prioritized in your relationship management strategy.

Deepening Relationships with the Relate Matrix

The true power of the Relate Matrix lies in its ability to help you deepen relationships. By understanding where each contact falls on the matrix, you can take intentional steps to enhance both the depth and transparency of your interactions.

1. **Assessing Current Relationships**: Start by plotting your key contacts on the Relate Matrix. Identify those with whom you have shallow or transactional relationships but would like to deepen the connection. Also, recognize those who are already close to you but where interactions could be more transparent.
2. **Setting Interaction Goals**: Based on your assessment, set specific goals for how to move relationships along the matrix. For example, if someone is an acquaintance but you'd like them to be a close friend, consider how you can increase both the frequency of your interactions and the level of transparency in your conversations.
3. **Determining Frequency of Interaction**: The Relate Matrix helps you determine how often you should interact with each contact to maintain or deepen the relationship. For example, casual friends might require a monthly check-in, while close friends and intimate friends might benefit from weekly or even daily interactions.
4. **Being Intentional**: Time and energy are limited, so the Relate Matrix helps you focus on the relationships that matter most. It guides you in making intentional decisions about where to invest your efforts, ensuring that you're not spreading yourself too thin.

The Benefits of a Well-Managed Network

By using the Relate Matrix, you can manage your 150 key relationships in a way that supports your personal and professional goals. This structured approach allows you to deepen meaningful connections, maintain essential contacts, and reduce the stress of trying to keep up with everyone all the time.

Fraternity—the relationships and networks we build—is a critical pillar of success. By understanding the limitations of your social capacity and using tools like the Relate Matrix, you can cultivate a network that not only supports you but also enriches your life in profound ways.

In the next chapter, we'll provide strategies for achieving financial stability and prosperity, a key pillar in your journey to sustained success. But for now, remember that the strength of your network isn't just about the number of contacts you have—it's about the quality and depth of the relationships you cultivate. The Relate Matrix is your guide to making those relationships as strong and fulfilling as they can be.

Relate Matrix

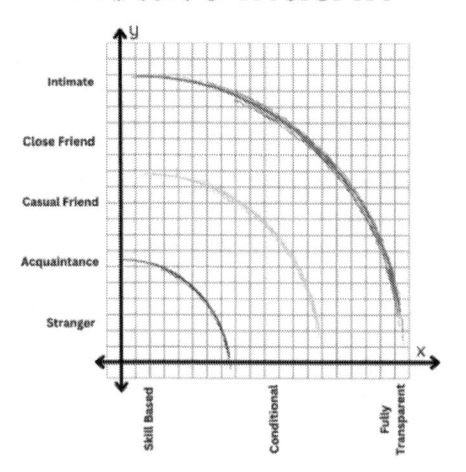

Chapter 12

Financial Well-Being

"Money is a terrible master but an excellent servant." - P.T. Barnum

Financial well-being is more than just having money in the bank—it's about creating a life where your finances support your goals, reduce stress, and provide the freedom to pursue what truly matters to you. While it might not be the most glamorous topic, financial well-being is a crucial pillar of a fulfilling life. Without it, even the best-laid plans can fall apart. This chapter explores how to cultivate financial health as the foundation of your overall success and happiness.

The Role of Financial Well-Being in Success

Money is often seen as a means to an end, but it's also a tool that can help you build the life you want. When your finances are in order, you have the freedom to make choices that align with your values and goals. You can invest in your health, spend time with loved ones, pursue passions, and give back to your community. Financial well-being provides stability and security, allowing you to focus on what really matters.

But financial well-being isn't just about earning more money—it's about managing what you have wisely. It's about understanding your financial situation, making informed decisions, and planning for the future. It's about creating a relationship with money that supports your overall well-being, rather than causing stress or anxiety.

Understanding Your Financial Situation

The first step toward financial well-being is gaining a clear understanding of your current financial situation. This means taking a close look at your income, expenses, debts, and savings. Many people avoid this step because it can be uncomfortable to confront financial realities, but it's essential if you want to take control of your financial future.

Start by creating a detailed budget that tracks all of your income and expenses. This will give you a clear picture of where your money is going and where you might need to make adjustments. Be honest with yourself about your spending habits and look for areas where you can cut back or reallocate funds to better align with your goals.

Once you have a clear understanding of your current situation, you can begin to make informed decisions about how to improve your financial health. This might involve paying down debt, increasing your savings, or investing in areas that will provide long-term returns.

Building a Strong Financial Foundation

Building a strong financial foundation involves more than just managing day-to-day expenses. It's about creating a plan that ensures your financial well-being for the long term. Here are some key steps to consider:

1. **Create an Emergency Fund**: One of the first steps in building financial security is to establish an emergency fund. This fund should cover at least three to six months of living expenses and be easily accessible in case of unexpected events, such as job loss, medical emergencies, or major repairs. Having an emergency fund provides peace of mind and protects you from

falling into debt when the unexpected happens.
2. **Pay Off High-Interest Debt**: High-interest debt, such as credit card balances, can be a significant drain on your finances. Prioritize paying off these debts as quickly as possible to free up resources for savings and investments. Consider consolidating debt or negotiating with creditors to lower interest rates, if possible.
3. **Save for Retirement**: It's never too early to start saving for retirement. Contribute to retirement accounts such as a 401(k), IRA, or other retirement savings plans, and take advantage of any employer matching contributions. The earlier you start, the more time your money has to grow through the power of compound interest.
4. **Invest Wisely**: Once you have an emergency fund and have addressed high-interest debt, consider investing in ways that align with your financial goals. This might include stocks, bonds, real estate, or other investment vehicles. Diversify your investments to spread risk and maximize potential returns. If you're unsure where to start, consider working with a financial advisor to create a personalized investment strategy.
5. **Protect Your Assets**: Ensure that you have adequate insurance coverage to protect yourself and your family from financial setbacks. This might include health insurance, life insurance, disability insurance, and property insurance. Review your policies regularly to make sure they continue to meet your needs.

Aligning Financial Decisions with Your Values

Financial well-being isn't just about accumulating wealth—it's about using your resources in ways that align with your values and contribute to your overall happiness. Consider how your financial decisions impact your quality of life, your relationships, and your long-term goals.

Ask yourself:

- **What are my core values, and how do they align with my financial goals?** For example, if you value security, you might prioritize building savings and paying off debt. If you value freedom, you might focus on creating passive income streams that allow you to work less and enjoy more leisure time.
- **How can I use my money to create a life that reflects what matters most to me?** This might involve investing in experiences that bring you joy, supporting causes you care about, or ensuring that your financial resources are used to build a legacy for future generations.

Creating a Financial Plan

A strong financial plan is a roadmap that guides your financial decisions and helps you stay on track to achieve your goals. Here's how to create one:

1. **Set Clear Financial Goals**: Start by setting clear, specific, and measurable financial goals. These could include paying off debt, saving for a down payment on a home, funding your children's education, or retiring early. Break these goals down into actionable steps and set timelines for achieving them.
2. **Monitor Your Progress**: Regularly review your financial plan to ensure you're making progress toward your goals. Adjust your plan as needed to account for changes in your income, expenses, or financial priorities.

3. **Seek Professional Advice**: Consider working with a financial advisor or planner to create a comprehensive financial plan tailored to your needs. A professional can help you navigate complex financial decisions, optimize your investments, and stay on track to achieve your goals.
4. **Stay Disciplined**: Financial success requires discipline and consistency. Stick to your budget, avoid unnecessary debt, and stay focused on your long-term goals. Remember that financial well-being is a journey, not a destination—it's about making smart choices every day that add up to a secure and fulfilling future.

The Freedom Financial Well-Being Brings

When your finances are in order, you gain more than just peace of mind—you gain the freedom to live life on your terms. Financial well-being gives you the ability to make choices that align with your values, pursue your passions, and create a life that reflects who you truly are. It allows you to focus on what matters most, without being weighed down by financial stress or uncertainty.

As you continue on your journey to success, remember that financial well-being is a crucial pillar. It's the foundation that supports all other aspects of your life, giving you the stability and security to achieve your goals and live a life of purpose and joy.

The next chapter will guide you through overcoming obstacles as you implement the F4 Framework in your life. But for now, take a moment to assess your financial health and consider how you can strengthen this foundation to support your future success.

Chapter 13

Overcoming Challenges in Implementing the F4

Implementing the F4 Framework—focused on Fitness, Focus, Fraternity, and Finance—can be a transformative journey, leading to profound personal and professional growth. However, like any meaningful change, it comes with its own set of challenges. As you embark on this journey, it's important to acknowledge and prepare for the obstacles that may arise, so you can navigate them effectively and stay on course.

Understanding the Common Challenges

Before diving into strategies for overcoming challenges, it's essential to understand the common obstacles that individuals face when implementing the F4 Framework. These challenges typically fall into a few key areas:

1. **Time Management**: Balancing the demands of fitness, focus, fraternity, and finance can feel overwhelming, especially when your schedule is already packed with personal and professional responsibilities.
2. **Consistency**: Building new habits and routines within each of the F4 pillars requires consistent effort. It's easy to lose momentum, especially when results aren't immediately visible.
3. **Mindset Shifts**: Implementing the F4 Framework often requires a shift in mindset—moving from reactive to proactive, from short-term to long-term thinking. This shift can be challenging, particularly if you've been

operating in a different mode for a long time.
4. **External Pressures**: Family, friends, and colleagues may not always understand or support the changes you're trying to make. External pressures can create doubt and make it harder to stay committed to your goals.
5. **Self-Doubt and Fear of Failure**: The fear of not being able to stick with the framework or the fear of failure can be significant barriers. These feelings can cause you to question your ability to succeed and lead to procrastination or giving up altogether.

As I worked through the challenges of implementing the F4 Framework, I noticed a troubling pattern in my self-talk. Whenever I faced setbacks or struggled to maintain consistency, I found myself saying, "I should be doing better," or "I should have figured this out by now." This kind of thinking didn't motivate me—it paralyzed me. That's when I realized I was "shoulding" on myself, and it was time to stop.

"Should" is a dangerous word. It implies that you're not enough as you are and that you're failing to meet some arbitrary standard. When you constantly tell yourself what you "should" be doing, you create a cycle of self-criticism that makes it harder to move forward.

To break this cycle, I started replacing "should" with more constructive language. Instead of saying, "I should have done better," I began saying, "I did the best I could with what I knew at the time, and now I can improve." This shift in mindset allowed me to approach challenges with curiosity rather than judgment, making it easier to learn from my experiences and keep progressing.

Embracing this mindset was a turning point in my journey with the F4 Framework. It helped me navigate the inevitable ups and downs with greater resilience and self-compassion, ensuring that I stayed on course even when things didn't go as planned.

Strategies for Overcoming Challenges

1. **Start Small and Prioritize**: One of the most effective ways to manage time and avoid overwhelm is to start small. Don't try to overhaul your entire life overnight. Instead, choose one or two areas of the F4 Framework to focus on first. Prioritize the pillar that resonates most with you or where you feel the greatest need for improvement. As you build momentum in that area, gradually incorporate the other pillars.
2. **Build Consistency with Micro Habits**: Consistency is key to success in any endeavor. To build consistency, start with micro habits—small, manageable actions that you can do daily without much effort. For example, if you're focusing on fitness, commit to just 5 minutes of exercise each morning. If it's finance, start by reviewing your budget for 5 minutes each day. These small actions will add up over time and help you build a solid foundation.
3. **Adopt a Growth Mindset**: Shifting your mindset is crucial for implementing the F4 Framework. Embrace a growth mindset, where challenges are seen as opportunities for learning and growth rather than obstacles. Recognize that setbacks are a natural part of the process and that each step, even the difficult ones, brings you closer to your goals.
4. **Seek Support and Communicate Your Goals**: External pressures can be tough to navigate, but you don't have to do it alone. Seek out support from those who understand and share your goals. This could be a mentor, a coach, or a community of like-minded individuals.

Communicate your goals to your close family and friends, explaining why these changes are important to you. Their understanding and support can make a significant difference in your journey.
5. **Address Self-Doubt with Action**: Self-doubt and fear of failure can be paralyzing, but the best way to overcome them is through action. Break down your goals into smaller, actionable steps, and focus on making progress rather than achieving perfection. Celebrate small wins along the way, and remind yourself that progress, no matter how small, is still progress. The act of moving forward, even in small steps, will build your confidence and help you overcome fear.

Learning from Setbacks

Setbacks are inevitable, but they don't have to derail your progress. When you encounter a challenge, take a moment to reflect on what happened, why it happened, and what you can learn from it. Use setbacks as learning opportunities to adjust your approach and strengthen your commitment.

For example, if you find that you've struggled to maintain your fitness routine, ask yourself why. Was it a lack of time, motivation, or resources? Once you identify the root cause, you can take steps to address it—whether that means adjusting your schedule, finding a workout buddy, or setting more realistic goals.

Remember, setbacks are not failures; they're simply feedback. They provide valuable insights that can help you refine your strategy and come back stronger.

Staying the Course

The journey of implementing the F4 Framework is not a sprint; it's a marathon. It requires patience, perseverance, and a commitment to long-term growth. Here are some tips for staying the course:

1. **Regularly Revisit Your Why**: Your motivation for implementing the F4 Framework should be deeply rooted in your personal values and long-term goals. Regularly revisit your "why" to remind yourself of the bigger picture and the impact these changes will have on your life.
2. **Track Your Progress**: Keeping track of your progress can provide a sense of accomplishment and keep you motivated. Whether it's through journaling, using a habit-tracking app, or setting up regular check-ins with yourself, find a way to measure and celebrate your progress.
3. **Be Kind to Yourself**: Change is hard, and it's important to be kind to yourself throughout the process. Recognize that there will be ups and downs, and that's okay. Give yourself permission to make mistakes, learn from them, and keep moving forward.
4. **Adjust as Needed**: The F4 Framework is a guide, not a rigid set of rules. As you progress, you may find that certain aspects of the framework need to be adjusted to better fit your life and goals. Be flexible and willing to adapt your approach as you learn what works best for you.

The Reward of Perseverance

The challenges of implementing the F4 Framework are real, but so are the rewards. As you overcome these obstacles, you'll find yourself growing stronger, more resilient, and more aligned with your true purpose. The habits you build, the mindset you cultivate, and the relationships you nurture will all contribute to a life that is not only successful but deeply fulfilling.

In the end, the F4 Framework isn't just about achieving specific goals—it's about creating a life that reflects your values, supports your well-being, and empowers you to reach your full potential. By facing and overcoming the challenges that arise, you'll develop the strength and wisdom needed to thrive in every area of your life.

In the next chapter, we'll explore how to maintain the progress you've made and continue to grow within the F4 Framework. But for now, take a moment to acknowledge the challenges you've faced and the progress you've made. Remember that every step forward, no matter how small, is a victory worth celebrating.

Chapter 14

The HAF+ Time Report:
Staying on Course

When I first set out to achieve my goals, I was full of energy and determination. I had my big-picture vision and a plan in place, but as the days turned into weeks, I noticed something unsettling—I was losing momentum. Despite my best intentions, I found myself drifting off course, struggling to keep up with the demands of my daily life while trying to stay focused on my long-term goals.

The Realization: I Needed a Weekly Check-In

It was during one particularly challenging week that I realized I needed a way to keep myself on track, not just on a monthly or quarterly basis, but every single week. The problem wasn't just that life was getting in the way—it was that I didn't have a consistent system to reflect on my progress, identify what was going wrong, and make real-time adjustments.

I had been setting ambitious goals, but without regular check-ins, I was often blindsided by obstacles or distractions that pulled me away from my path. I needed a way to pause, reflect, and course-correct before small issues became major roadblocks.

The Birth of the HAF+ Time Report

This realization led me to develop what I now call the HAF+ Time Report. It's a process designed to do exactly what I needed—help me stay on course, week by week, by reflecting on my experiences and making the necessary adjustments.

The idea was simple: each week, I would ask myself three key questions:

1. **Hurdles**: What obstacles did I encounter this week that slowed me down or prevented me from making progress?
2. **Ahas**: What insights or realizations did I have that could help me improve moving forward?
3. **Fixes**: What solutions did I implement to overcome these hurdles or capitalize on these insights?

And then, to round it all out, I'd add a "+" to the process—a commitment to set specific goals for the upcoming week in each of the four pillars of my life: Fitness, Focus, Fraternity, and Finance. This would ensure that I wasn't just reflecting on the past, but actively planning for the future.

The First HAF+ Report: A New Level of Awareness

The first time I sat down to complete a HAF+ Time Report, it was like a light bulb went off in my head. As I reflected on the hurdles I had faced that week, I saw patterns I hadn't noticed before—recurring challenges that were subtly undermining my efforts.

For example, I realized that my fitness goals were consistently being pushed aside because I hadn't set clear boundaries around my workout time. I also noticed that my focus was wavering because I wasn't prioritizing my tasks effectively—I was letting less important activities eat up time that should have been dedicated to my most critical goals.

But the real magic happened when I started identifying the "ahas"—those moments of clarity that often go unnoticed in the rush of daily life. I realized that my biggest breakthroughs often came from small adjustments—tweaking my morning routine, adjusting my work environment, or simply changing my mindset.

With these insights in hand, I moved on to the "fixes," implementing practical solutions to address the hurdles I'd encountered. I started setting firm boundaries around my fitness time, prioritizing my tasks more effectively, and making small but impactful changes to my daily routine.

Finally, I set my goals for the upcoming week, making sure they were aligned with the bigger picture and that they addressed the areas where I had struggled the most. This simple, weekly process gave me a new level of awareness and control over my progress.

The Impact: Staying the Course, Week After Week

As I continued to use the HAF+ Time Report, I found that it not only helped me stay on track but also made me more resilient. By regularly reflecting on my experiences and making adjustments, I was able to bounce back more quickly from setbacks and keep moving forward, no matter what challenges came my way.

Over time, the HAF+ Time Report became a cornerstone of my goal-setting process. It's what allows me to stay the course, week after week, and make steady progress toward my 30-day and 90-day plans. Even when life throws unexpected hurdles my way, the HAF+ process helps me stay grounded, focused, and committed to my goals.

The HAF+ Process: Breaking It Down

Here's how the HAF+ Time Report works, step by step:

Hurdles: Reflect on the past week and identify the obstacles that slowed you down or got in your way.

Hurdles
(List the challenges faced this week)

Ahas: Consider the key insights or realizations you had during the week. What did you learn that can help you improve?

Ahas
(Insights gained this week)

Fixes: Document the solutions or actions you took to overcome the hurdles or make use of your insights.

Fixes
(Actions taken this week)

Set Goals for the Upcoming Week: Use what you've learned to set specific, actionable goals for the next week in each of the four pillars of your life: Fitness, Focus, Fraternity, and Finance.

Pillar	Weekly Goal
Fitness	(Goal for fitness)
Focus	(Goal for focus)
Fraternity	(Goal for relationships)
Finance	(Goal for finances)

Even with the HAF+ Time Report keeping me on track each week, I found that there were times when I couldn't see the progress I was making. I needed something more tangible—a way to measure my daily efforts and keep my momentum going. That's when I created the Weekly Momentum Scorecard.

The scorecard was a simple chart that tracked my daily progress toward my weekly goals. I listed my goals down one side and the days of the week across the top. Each day, I'd mark off my accomplishments: Did I complete my workout? Did I make that important call? Did I stick to my meditation practice? Seeing those marks accumulate throughout the week gave me a visual sense of progress that kept me motivated.

But the scorecard wasn't just about checking off tasks. I

added three more columns at the bottom: Hurdles, Ahas, and Fixes. Each day, I'd jot down the obstacles I encountered, the insights I gained, and the solutions I implemented. This reflection helped me identify patterns and adjust my approach in real time.

By the end of the week, I had a clear picture of my momentum. The scorecard wasn't just a record of what I did—it was a tool for learning, adapting, and staying motivated. It kept me accountable to my goals and reminded me that every small step forward was building toward something bigger.

The Power of Consistency

The HAF+ Time Report isn't just about reflection—it's about creating a consistent habit of self-assessment and adjustment. By dedicating time each week to this process, I've been able to stay on track and make meaningful progress toward my long-term goals.

This process is now an integral part of my journey. It's how I ensure that I'm not just busy, but productive; not just moving, but moving in the right direction. And it's how I've learned to stay the course, even when the path gets challenging.

Chapter 15

The Journey to M.A.P. - Finding the Right Course

In the pursuit of my goals, I quickly realized that the path to success isn't always a straight line. Early on, I often found myself either overcommitting or underestimating the time and resources needed to reach my targets. As weeks passed, I'd notice the gap between where I thought I'd be and where I actually was growing wider. Something had to change.

The Realization: Weekly Check-Ins Weren't Enough

I had already developed the HAF+ Time Report, a weekly check-in tool that helped me reflect on my short-term progress. This was a game changer in keeping me focused on my immediate tasks and goals. But as I reviewed my HAF+ reports week after week, I noticed a pattern—while I was staying on track in the short term, my broader goals for the month, and especially for the 90-day period, weren't aligning as closely as I wanted.

There were moments when I thought I was making steady progress, only to find that I wasn't as close to my 90-day goals as I had hoped. It became clear that while weekly monitoring was vital, it wasn't enough to course-correct on a larger scale. I needed something more comprehensive—a way to assess my entire month and make strategic adjustments.

The Birth of M.A.P.: A Monthly Reflection

It was after one particularly challenging month that I realized the missing piece: I wasn't just missing regular assessment; I was missing a deeper understanding of how my mindset, abilities, and performance were influencing my progress. This insight led me to create what I now call the M.A.P. process—Mindset, Ability, and Performance.

I started experimenting with this new approach by taking the last day of each month to pause and look back over the previous four weeks. But instead of just revisiting the details of my weekly HAF+ reports, I asked myself three critical questions:

1. **Mindset**: How was my mindset this month, both personally and professionally? Was I feeling motivated and focused, or was I letting stress and doubt creep in?
2. **Ability**: Did I have the necessary skills, tools, and support to accomplish my goals? Where was I strong, and where did I struggle?
3. **Performance**: How effective was I in executing my plans? Did I achieve what I set out to do, or did I fall short? If I fell short, why?

These questions forced me to take a hard look at not just what I was doing, but how I was approaching my work and life. They provided the clarity I needed to see why I was either succeeding or struggling and what adjustments I needed to make.

The First M.A.P.: A New Path Forward

The first time I used M.A.P., the results were eye-opening. I saw clearly that my mindset had been overly cautious—I was holding back from taking bigger risks because I was afraid of failing. My ability to execute was hampered by a lack of specific tools that I had neglected to acquire, thinking I could get by without them. And my performance, while steady, wasn't as impactful as I wanted it to be because I wasn't fully committing to my goals.

With this new understanding, I made adjustments. I shifted my mindset by embracing a more adventurous approach, similar to what I did with my Vision Builder's "Reach" goals. I invested in the tools I needed and sought out additional support from my network. Finally, I revamped my upcoming 30-day plan to reflect these changes, setting bolder, more ambitious targets that would push me closer to my 90-day goals.

Refining the Process: Monthly Adjustments

As I continued using M.A.P. each month, it became clear that this process wasn't just about reflection—it was about strategic adjustment. Every month, I'd look back at my mindset, ability, and performance and make tweaks to my upcoming 30-day plan. This allowed me to stay agile, responsive, and always moving forward, even when challenges arose.

I found that by regularly assessing my progress and making informed adjustments, I was able to close the gap between my short-term actions and my long-term vision. The M.A.P. process became an integral part of my success strategy, ensuring that I wasn't just busy, but truly productive and aligned with my highest goals.

The M.A.P. Process: A Closer Look

Here's how I now approach the M.A.P. process each month:

Mindset: Reflect on how my thoughts, emotions, and attitudes have influenced my progress. Am I thinking big enough? Am I maintaining the positive, growth-oriented mindset that will propel me forward?

Mindset	Reflection
Personal	(How was your personal mindset?)
Professional	(How was your professional mindset?)

Ability: Evaluate whether I had the right skills, tools, and support. Did I have everything I needed to succeed, or were there gaps that held me back?

Ability	Reflection
Skills	(Were your skills adequate?)
Tools	(Did you have the right tools?)
Support	(Was your team supportive?)

Performance: Review my execution and outcomes. Did I meet my goals? If not, why? What can I do better next month?

Performance	Reflection
Execution	(How effective was your execution?)
Outcomes	(Did you achieve your goals?)

Moving Forward: Adjusting the 30-Day Plan

With these insights, I adjust my upcoming 30-day plan to align more closely with my overall 90-day goals. This ensures that I'm constantly refining my approach, staying agile, and responding to the realities of my progress.

Pillar	New 30-Day Goal
Fitness	(Adjusted goal for fitness)
Focus	(Adjusted goal for focus)
Fraternity	(Adjusted goal for relationships)
Finance	(Adjusted goal for finances)

Finally, at the end of each 90-day cycle, I revisit the Vision Builder process, redefining my goals and recalibrating my strategy for the next phase. This ongoing cycle of reflection, adjustment, and forward momentum has been key to not only reaching my goals but often exceeding them.

Chapter 16

Sustaining Long-Term Success with the F4 Framework

Achieving success is one thing, but sustaining it over the long term is another. The F4 Framework—focused on Fitness, Focus, Fraternity, and Finance—provides a holistic approach to building a life of purpose, balance, and fulfillment. But once you've implemented the framework and started seeing results, how do you ensure that success continues? How do you maintain the momentum, avoid burnout, and keep growing? This chapter explores the strategies and mindset needed to sustain long-term success with the F4 Framework.

The Importance of Consistency

Consistency is the bedrock of sustained success. The habits and routines you've established within each pillar of the F4 Framework are what drive continuous growth and improvement. However, consistency doesn't mean rigidity—it's about maintaining your commitment to the principles of the framework while being adaptable to change.

One of the most important aspects of consistency is making the F4 Framework a part of your daily life, rather than something you do only when it's convenient. This means regularly engaging in the practices that support your fitness, focus, relationships, and financial health. Whether it's daily exercise, meditation, networking, or financial planning, these activities need to become ingrained in your routine.

But consistency isn't just about repetition; it's also about quality. Ensure that the time you dedicate to each pillar is intentional and aligned with your goals. It's better to have a focused, productive 20-minute workout than a distracted hour at the gym. Quality over quantity is key to maintaining long-term success.

Adapting to Life's Changes

Life is dynamic, and sustaining long-term success requires flexibility and adaptability. As you progress, your circumstances, goals, and priorities will inevitably change. The F4 Framework is designed to be flexible, allowing you to adjust your approach as needed while still adhering to the core principles.

For example, as your career evolves, you may find that your focus needs to shift from building new relationships to deepening existing ones. Or perhaps your financial goals will change from paying off debt to investing in new opportunities. The key is to regularly assess where you are and where you want to go, and to adapt your strategies accordingly.

Adapting to change also means being prepared for setbacks. Life will throw challenges your way—whether it's a health issue, a financial setback, or a personal loss. These challenges can disrupt your routine and make it difficult to stay on track. But by staying grounded in the F4 Framework, you'll have the tools and mindset to navigate these difficulties and get back on course.

Continuous Learning and Growth

Sustaining long-term success also requires a commitment to continuous learning and growth. The world is constantly changing, and staying ahead means being open to new ideas, skills, and perspectives. The F4 Framework encourages you to embrace a growth mindset—where you see challenges as opportunities to learn and improve.

To keep growing, make it a habit to regularly seek out new knowledge and experiences. This could mean attending workshops, reading books, seeking mentorship, or exploring new hobbies. Continuously expanding your horizons will not only keep you engaged and motivated, but it will also enhance your ability to adapt to new situations and seize opportunities as they arise.

Growth isn't just about accumulating knowledge—it's also about applying what you learn. Take the insights you gain and integrate them into your life and work. Experiment with new approaches, refine your strategies, and don't be afraid to step out of your comfort zone. Growth happens at the edge of discomfort, so embrace the challenges that come with pushing your boundaries.

Maintaining Balance and Avoiding Burnout

One of the biggest threats to long-term success is burnout. It's easy to get caught up in the pursuit of goals and lose sight of the need for balance and self-care. The F4 Framework is designed to help you maintain that balance by addressing all aspects of your life—physical, mental, emotional, and financial.

To avoid burnout, it's important to regularly check in with yourself and assess your well-being across all four pillars. Are you feeling physically exhausted? Are you mentally overwhelmed? Are your relationships suffering because you're too focused on work? These are signs that you may need to re-balance your priorities.

Self-care is not a luxury; it's a necessity for sustaining success. This means taking time to rest, recharge, and engage in activities that bring you joy. It also means setting boundaries to protect your time and energy. Remember that you can't pour from an empty cup—taking care of yourself is essential for taking care of everything else.

The Power of Reflection

Reflection is a powerful tool for sustaining long-term success. By regularly reflecting on your progress, you can celebrate your achievements, learn from your mistakes, and stay aligned with your goals. The F4 Framework encourages you to build reflection into your routine—whether it's through journaling, meditation, or simply taking a few minutes each day to think about what's working and what's not.

Reflection allows you to course-correct when needed and to stay connected to your "why." It's a reminder of why you started this journey in the first place and the impact you want to make. Regular reflection helps you stay motivated, focused, and committed to the path you've chosen.

Building a Legacy

Ultimately, sustaining long-term success with the F4 Framework is about more than just achieving personal goals—it's about building a legacy. The habits, relationships, and impact you create through the framework will extend beyond your own life, influencing others and leaving a lasting mark.

Consider how you can use the principles of the F4

Framework to contribute to your community, mentor others, and create positive change. By sharing what you've learned and supporting others on their journey, you not only reinforce your own success but also help build a better world.

Conclusion: A Life of Sustained Success

The F4 Framework provides a comprehensive approach to achieving and sustaining long-term success. By focusing on fitness, focus, fraternity, and finance, you create a balanced and fulfilling life that supports your goals and values. But sustaining that success requires ongoing effort, adaptability, and a commitment to continuous growth.

As you move forward, remember that success is not a destination—it's a journey. The habits and practices you cultivate today will shape your future and determine the legacy you leave behind. Stay consistent, stay adaptable, and stay true to the principles of the F4 Framework. In doing so, you'll not only achieve your goals but also create a life of lasting impact and fulfillment.

Acknowledgement

This book is more than just a collection of strategies and ideas; it's a reflection of my personal journey toward balance, growth, and fulfillment through the F4 Framework—Fitness, Focus, Fraternity, and Finance. I couldn't have completed this journey, or this book, without the support, encouragement, and patience of the incredible people in my life.

First and foremost, I want to express my deepest gratitude to my wife, DaniElle, and our children, Ava, Wil, and Grey. You have given me the space, time, and encouragement to write this book, try out new theories, and pursue my vision with unwavering support. DaniElle, your belief in me has been my anchor, and your partnership in both life and work has made this journey possible. Ava, Will, and Grey, thank you for your love, patience, and understanding as I dedicated countless hours to this project. Your presence has been a constant reminder of why this work matters.

I am also deeply grateful to Syl, my personal assistant, whose dedication and organizational skills have kept me focused and on track. Your ability to manage the details allowed me to concentrate on developing and refining the F4 Framework. Your support has been crucial in bringing this project to life.

Finally, to all the clients, friends, and readers who have shared their stories, challenges, and successes with me—thank you. Your journeys have enriched my understanding of the F4 Framework and inspired me to continue refining and sharing these principles. This book is as much yours as it is mine, and I am honored to be part of your path to fulfillment and success.

Writing this handbook has been a transformative experience, one that has deepened my commitment to living a life of balance and purpose. I hope that the principles and practices shared within these pages will inspire you to embark on your own journey toward total fulfillment. Thank you for being a part of this process, and I look forward to seeing where your journey takes you.

With deep gratitude,

David Wible

Made in the USA
Middletown, DE
16 February 2025

71022186R10052